www.osha.gov

This best practices guide is not a standard or regulation, and it creates no new legal obligations, nor does it change any existing OSHA standard or regulation. The guide is advisory in nature, informational in content, and is intended to assist employers in providing a safe and healthful workplace.

The Occupational Safety and Health Act of 1970 (OSH Act) requires employers to comply with hazard-specific safety and health standards and regulations as issued and enforced by either the Federal Occupational Safety and Health Administration (OSHA), or an OSHA-approved State Plan. In addition, employers must provide their employees with a workplace free from recognized hazards likely to cause death or serious physical harm under Section 5(a)(1), the General Duty Clause of the Act. Employers can be cited for violating the General Duty Clause if there is a recognized hazard and they do not take steps to prevent or abate the hazard. However, failure to implement this guide is not, in itself, a violation of the General Duty Clause. Citations can only be based on standards, regulations, and the General Duty Clause.

Best Practices Guide:
Fundamentals of a Workplace First-Aid Program

U.S. Department of Labor

Occupational Safety and Health Administration

OSHA 3317-06N
2006

Contents

Introduction and Purpose . . . 3

The Risks: Injuries, Illnesses and Fatalities . . . 4

Assess the Risks and Design a First-Aid Program Specific for the Worksite . . . 5

OSHA Requirements . . . 8

First-Aid Supplies . . . 9

Automated External Defibrillators . . . 10

First-Aid Courses . . . 11

Elements of a First-Aid Training Program . . . 11

Trainee Assessment . . . 15

Skills Update . . . 15

Program Update . . . 15

Summary . . . 16

Additional Resources on First Aid, CPR and AEDs . . . 16

References . . . 17

OSHA Assistance . . . 18

OSHA Regional Offices . . . 23

Introduction and Purpose

First aid is emergency care provided for injury or sudden illness before emergency medical treatment is available. The first-aid provider in the workplace is someone who is trained in the delivery of initial medical emergency procedures, using a limited amount of equipment to perform a primary assessment and intervention while awaiting arrival of emergency medical service (EMS) personnel.

A workplace first-aid program is part of a comprehensive safety and health management system that includes the following four essential elements[1]:

- Management Leadership and Employee Involvement
- Worksite Analysis
- Hazard Prevention and Control
- Safety and Health Training

The purpose of this guide is to present a summary of the basic elements for a first-aid program at the workplace. Those elements include:

- Identifying and assessing the workplace risks that have potential to cause worker injury or illness.
- Designing and implementing a workplace first-aid program that:
  - Aims to minimize the outcome of accidents or exposures
  - Complies with OSHA requirements relating to first aid
  - Includes sufficient quantities of appropriate and readily accessible first-aid supplies and first-aid equipment, such as bandages and automated external defibrillators.
  - Assigns and trains first-aid providers who:
    - receive first-aid training suitable to the specific workplace
    - receive periodic refresher courses on first-aid skills and knowledge.

[1] CSP 03-01-002 - TED 8.4 - Voluntary Protection Programs (VPP): Policies and Procedures Manual Notice. 54 Federal Register 3904-3916. Available at www.osha.gov/pls/oshaweb/owadisp.show_document?p_table=DIRECTIVES&p_id =2976

3

- Instructing all workers about the first-aid program, including what workers should do if a coworker is injured or ill. Putting the policies and program in writing is recommended to implement this and other program elements.
- Providing for scheduled evaluation and changing of the first-aid program to keep the program current and applicable to emerging risks in the workplace, including regular assessment of the adequacy of the first-aid training course.

This guide also includes an outline of the essential elements of safe and effective first-aid training for the workplace as guidance to institutions teaching first-aid courses and to the consumers of these courses.

The Risks: Injuries, Illnesses and Fatalities

There were 5,703 work-related fatalities in private industry in 2004. In that same year there were 4.3 million total workplace injuries and illnesses, of which 1.3 million resulted in days away from work.

Occupational illnesses, injuries and fatalities in 2004 cost the United States' economy $142.2 billion, according to National Safety Council estimates. The average cost per occupational fatality in 2004 exceeded one million dollars. To cover the costs to employers from workplace injuries, it has been calculated that each and every employee in this country would have had to generate $1,010 in revenue in 2004.[2]

Sudden cardiac arrest (SCA) may occur at work. According to recent statistics from the American Heart Association, there are 250,000 out-of-hospital SCAs annually. The actual number of SCAs that happen at work are unknown. If an employee collapses without warning and is not attended to promptly and effectively, the employee may die. Sudden cardiac arrest is caused by abnormal, uncoordinated beating of the heart or loss of the heartbeat altogether, usually as a result of a heart attack.

[2] National Safety Council. (2006). *Injury Facts,* 2004 - 2006 Edition. Itasca, IL, p. 51.

Workplace events such as electrocution or exposure to low oxygen environments can lead to SCA. Overexertion at work can also trigger SCA in those with underlying heart disease.

The outcome of occupational illnesses and injuries depends on the severity of the injury, available first-aid care and medical treatment. Prompt, properly administered first aid may mean the difference between rapid or prolonged recovery, temporary or permanent disability, and even life or death.

Assess the Risks and Design a First-Aid Program Specific for the Worksite

Obtaining and evaluating information about the injuries, illnesses and fatalities at a worksite are essential first steps in planning a first-aid program. Employers can use the OSHA 300 log, OSHA 301 forms, their Workers' Compensation insurance carrier reports or other records to help identify the first-aid needs for their businesses. For risk assessment purposes, national data for injuries, illnesses and fatalities may be obtained from the Bureau of Labor Statistics (BLS) website at www.bls.gov/iif. The annual data, beginning in 2003, are grouped by the North American Industrial Classification System (NAICS) that assigns a numeric code for each type of work establishment. Prior to 2003, the Standard Industrial Classification (SIC) system was used to categorize the data instead of NAICS.

The graphs that follow provide examples of fatality, injury and illness analyses that can be developed using BLS data.

Figure 1 shows the distribution by NAICS sector of workplace fatalities that occurred in private industry in 2004, the most recent year for which data was available.

Figure 1. Percent Fatalities in Private Industry by NAICS Sector, 2004

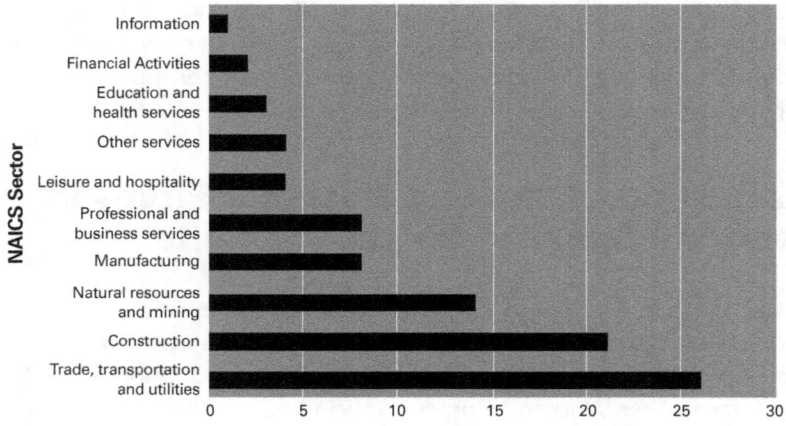

Percent Fatalities of 5,703 total fatalities
Note: The total includes fatalities that occurred in the public sector; therefore, the percentages above do not add up to 100.

The categories of events or exposures responsible for workplace fatalities in 2004 are shown in Figure 2. More detailed data are available from the BLS website.

Figure 2. Occupational Fatalities by Event or Exposure, 2004

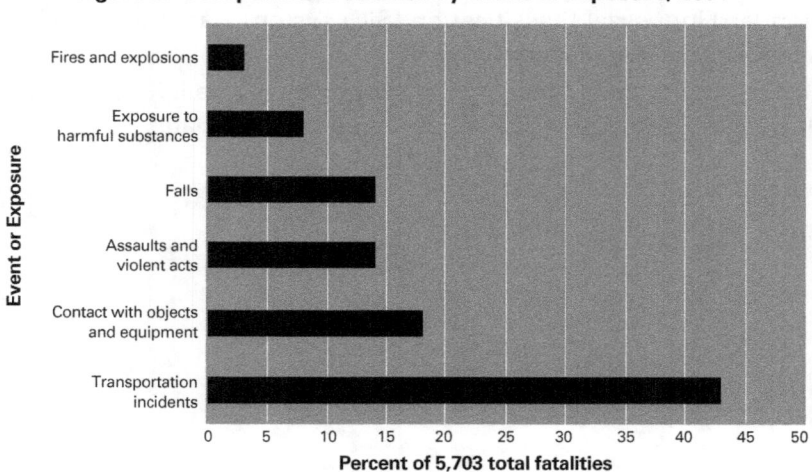

Percent of 5,703 total fatalities

Figure 3 reflects total injuries and illnesses by NAICS sector based on 2004 BLS data. Data that are more specific to businesses within these sectors may be obtained from the BLS website.

Figure 3. Number of Recordable Injuries and Illnesses by NAICS Sector, 2004

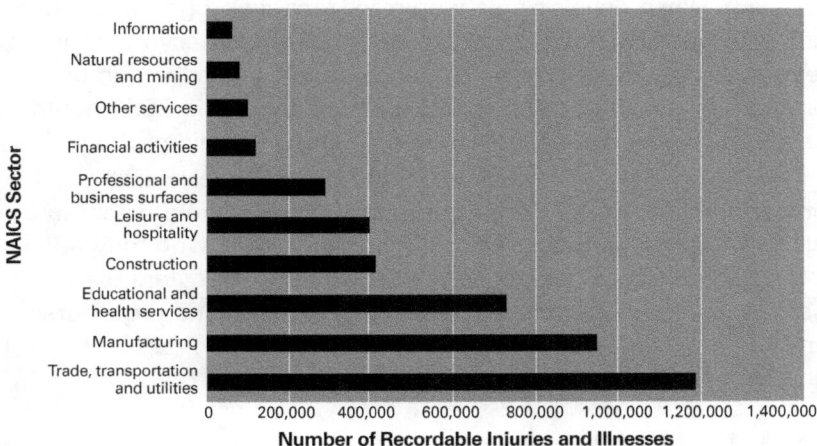

The graph in Figure 4 shows the number of injuries and illnesses in private industry by the type of event or exposure responsible for them that resulted in days away from work in 2004. More detailed data may be found on the BLS website.

Figure 4. Private Industry Injuries and Illnesses Involving Days Away from Work per 10,000 Employees by Event or Exposure, 2004

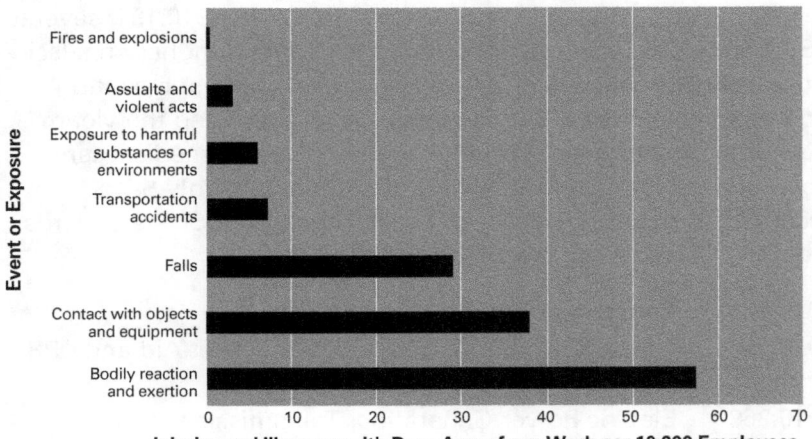

Employers should make an effort to obtain estimates of EMS response times for all permanent and temporary locations and for all times of the day and night at which they have workers on duty, and they should use that information when planning their first-aid program. When developing a workplace first-aid program, consultation with the local fire and rescue service or emergency medical professionals may be helpful for response time information and other program issues. Because it can be a workplace event, SCA should be considered by employers when planning a first-aid program.

It is advisable to put the First-Aid Program policies and procedures in writing. Policies and procedures should be communicated to all employees, including those workers who may not read or speak English. Language barriers should be addressed both in instructing employees on first-aid policies and procedures and when designating individuals who will receive first-aid training and become the on-site first-aid providers.

OSHA Requirements

Sudden injuries or illnesses, some of which may be life-threatening, occur at work. The OSHA First Aid standard (29 CFR 1910.151) requires trained first-aid providers at all workplaces of any size if there is no "infirmary, clinic, or hospital in near proximity to the workplace which is used for the treatment of all injured employees."

In addition to first-aid requirements of 29 CFR 1910.151, several OSHA standards also require training in cardiopulmonary resuscitation (CPR) because sudden cardiac arrest from asphyxiation, electrocution, or exertion may occur. CPR may keep the victim alive until EMS arrives to provide the next level of medical care. However, survival from this kind of care is low, only 5-7%, according to the American Heart Association. The OSHA standards requiring CPR training are:

1910.146	Permit-required Confined Spaces
1910.266	Appendix B: Logging Operations – First-Aid and CPR Training
1910.269	Electric Power Generation, Transmission, and Distribution

1910.410   Qualifications of Dive Team

1926.950   Construction Subpart V, Power Transmission and
            Distribution

If an employee is expected to render first aid as part of his or her job duties, the employee is covered by the requirements of the Occupational Exposure to Bloodborne Pathogens standard (29 CFR 1910.1030). This standard includes specific training requirements.

A few of the medical emergency procedures mentioned in this guide as first aid may be considered *medical treatment* for OSHA recordkeeping purposes. The OSHA Recording and Reporting Occupational Injuries and Illnesses regulation (29 CFR 1904) provides specific definitions of *first aid and medical treatment.* If a medical emergency procedure which is considered by 29 CFR 1904 to be medical treatment is performed on an employee with an occupational injury or illness, then the injury or illness will be regarded as recordable on the OSHA 300 Log.

First-Aid Supplies

It is advisable for the employer to give a specific person the responsibility for choosing the types and amounts of first-aid supplies and for maintaining these supplies. The supplies must be adequate, should reflect the kinds of injuries that occur, and must be stored in an area where they are readily available for emergency access. An automated external defibrillator (AED) should be considered when selecting first-aid supplies and equipment.

A specific example of the minimal contents of a workplace first-aid kit is described in American National Standards Institute ANSI Z308.1 - 2003, *Minimum Requirements for Workplace First Aid Kits.* The kits described are suitable for small businesses. For large operations, employers should determine how many first-aid kits are needed, and if it is appropriate to augment the kits with additional first-aid equipment and supplies.

Employers who have unique or changing first-aid needs should consider upgrading their first-aid kits. The employer can use the OSHA 300 log, OSHA 301 reports or other records to identify the first-aid supply needs of their worksite. Consultation with the local

fire and rescue service or emergency medical professionals may be beneficial. By assessing the specific needs of their workplaces, employers can ensure the availability of adequate first-aid supplies. Employers should periodically reassess the demand for these supplies and adjust their inventories.

Automated External Defibrillators

With recent advances in technology, automated external defibrillators (AEDs) are now widely available, safe, effective, portable, and easy to use. They provide the critical and necessary treatment for sudden cardiac arrest (SCA) caused by ventricular fibrillation, the uncoordinated beating of the heart leading to collapse and death. Using AEDs as soon as possible after sudden cardiac arrest, within 3-4 minutes, can lead to a 60% survival rate.[3] CPR is of value because it supports the circulation and ventilation of the victim until an electric shock delivered by an AED can restore the fibrillating heart to normal.

All worksites are potential candidates for AED programs because of the possibility of SCA and the need for timely defibrillation. Each workplace should assess its own requirements for an AED program as part of its first-aid response.

A number of issues should be considered in setting up a worksite AED program: physician oversight; compliance with local, state and federal regulations; coordination with local EMS; a quality assurance program; and a periodic review, among others. The OSHA website at www.osha.gov or the websites of the American College of Occupational and Environmental Medicine at www.acoem.org, the American Heart Association at www.americanheart.org, the American Red Cross at www.redcross.org, Federal Occupational Health at www.foh.dhhs.gov, and the National Center for Early Defibrillation at www.early-defib.org can provide additional information about AED program development.

[3] American Heart Association in collaboration with International Liaison Committee on Resuscitation. *Guidelines 2000 for Cardiopulmonary Resuscitation and Emergency Cardiovascular Care: International Consensus on Science, Part 4: The Automated External Defibrillator.* Circulation. 2000; Vol. 102, Supplement: I 61. Figure 1.

First-Aid Courses

Training for first aid is offered by the American Heart Association, the American Red Cross, the National Safety Council, and other nationally recognized and private educational organizations. OSHA does not teach first-aid courses or certify first-aid training courses for instructors or trainees.

First-aid courses should be individualized to the needs of the workplace. Some of the noted program elements may be optional for a particular plant or facility. On the other hand, unique conditions at a specific worksite may necessitate the addition of customized elements to a first-aid training program.

Elements of a First-Aid Training Program

There are a number of elements to include when planning a first-aid training program for a particular workplace. These recommendations are based on the best practices and evidence available at the time this guide was written. Statistical information is available from BLS to help assess the risks for specific types of work. Program elements to be considered are:

1. Teaching Methods

Training programs should incorporate the following principles:
- Basing the curriculum on a consensus of scientific evidence where available;
- Having trainees develop "hands-on" skills through the use of mannequins and partner practice;
- Having appropriate first-aid supplies and equipment available;
- Exposing trainees to acute injury and illness settings as well as to the appropriate response through the use of visual aids;
- Including a course information resource for reference both during and after training;
- Allowing enough time for emphasis on commonly occurring situations;
- Emphasizing skills training and confidence-building over classroom lectures;
- Emphasizing quick response to first-aid situations.

2. Preparing to Respond to a Health Emergency

The training program should include instruction or discussion in the following:

- Prevention as a strategy in reducing fatalities, illnesses and injuries;
- Interacting with the local EMS system;
- Maintaining a current list of emergency telephone numbers (police, fire, ambulance, poison control) accessible by all employees;
- Understanding the legal aspects of providing first-aid care, including Good Samaritan legislation, consent, abandonment, negligence, assault and battery, State laws and regulations;
- Understanding the effects of stress, fear of infection, panic; how they interfere with performance; and what to do to overcome these barriers to action;
- Learning the importance of universal precautions and body substance isolation to provide protection from bloodborne pathogens and other potentially infectious materials. Learning about personal protective equipment -- gloves, eye protection, masks, and respiratory barrier devices. Appropriate management and disposal of blood-contaminated sharps and surfaces; and awareness of OSHA's Bloodborne Pathogens standard.

3. Assessing the Scene and the Victim(s)

The training program should include instruction in the following:

- Assessing the scene for safety, number of injured, and nature of the event;
- Assessing the toxic potential of the environment and the need for respiratory protection;
- Establishing the presence of a confined space and the need for respiratory protection and specialized training to perform a rescue;
- Prioritizing care when there are several injured;
- Assessing each victim for responsiveness, airway patency (blockage), breathing, circulation, and medical alert tags;
- Taking a victim's history at the scene, including determining the mechanism of injury;
- Performing a logical head-to-toe check for injuries;

- Stressing the need to continuously monitor the victim;
- Emphasizing early activation of EMS;
- Indications for and methods of safely moving and rescuing victims;
- Repositioning ill/injured victims to prevent further injury.

4. Responding to Life-Threatening Emergencies

The training program should be designed or adapted for the specific worksite and may include first-aid instruction in the following:

- Establishing responsiveness;
- Establishing and maintaining an open and clear airway;
- Performing rescue breathing;
- Treating airway obstruction in a conscious victim;
- Performing CPR;
- Using an AED;
- Recognizing the signs and symptoms of shock and providing first aid for shock due to illness or injury;
- Assessing and treating a victim who has an unexplained change in level of consciousness or sudden illness;
- Controlling bleeding with direct pressure;
- Poisoning
  - Ingested poisons: alkali, acid, and systemic poisons. Role of the Poison Control Center (1-800-222-1222);
  - Inhaled poisons: carbon monoxide; hydrogen sulfide; smoke; and other chemical fumes, vapors, and gases. Assessing the toxic potential of the environment and the need for respirators;
  - Knowledge of the chemicals at the worksite and of first aid and treatment for inhalation or ingestion;
  - Effects of alcohol and illicit drugs so that the first-aid provider can recognize the physiologic and behavioral effects of these substances.
- Recognizing asphyxiation and the danger of entering a confined space without appropriate respiratory protection. Additional training is required if first-aid personnel will assist in the rescue from the confined space.
- Responding to Medical Emergencies
  - Chest pain;

- Stroke;
- Breathing problems;
- Anaphylactic reaction;
- Hypoglycemia in diabetics taking insulin;
- Seizures;
- Pregnancy complications;
- Abdominal injury;
- Reduced level of consciousness;
- Impaled object.

5. Responding to Non-Life-Threatening Emergencies

The training program should be designed for the specific worksite and include first-aid instruction for the management of the following:

- Wounds
  - Assessment and first aid for wounds including abrasions, cuts, lacerations, punctures, avulsions, amputations and crush injuries;
  - Principles of wound care, including infection precautions;
  - Principles of body substance isolation, universal precautions and use of personal protective equipment.
- Burns
  - Assessing the severity of a burn;
  - Recognizing whether a burn is thermal, electrical, or chemical and the appropriate first aid;
  - Reviewing corrosive chemicals at a specific worksite, along with appropriate first aid.
- Temperature Extremes
  - Exposure to cold, including frostbite and hypothermia;
  - Exposure to heat, including heat cramps, heat exhaustion and heat stroke.
- Musculoskeletal Injuries
  - Fractures;
  - Sprains, strains, contusions and cramps;
  - Head, neck, back and spinal injuries;
  - Appropriate handling of amputated body parts.
- Eye injuries
  - First aid for eye injuries;

- First aid for chemical burns.
■ Mouth and Teeth Injuries
  - Oral injuries; lip and tongue injuries; broken and missing teeth;
  - The importance of preventing aspiration of blood and/or teeth.
■ Bites and Stings
  - Human and animal bites;
  - Bites and stings from insects; instruction in first-aid treatment of anaphylactic shock.

Trainee Assessment

Assessment of successful completion of the first-aid training program should include instructor observation of acquired skills and written performance assessments.

Skills Update

First-aid responders may have long intervals between learning and using CPR and AED skills. Numerous studies have shown a retention rate of 6-12 months of these critical skills. The American Heart Association's Emergency Cardiovascular Care Committee encourages skills review and practice sessions at least every 6 months for CPR and AED skills. Instructor-led retraining for life-threatening emergencies should occur at least annually. Retraining for non-life-threatening response should occur periodically.

Program Update

The first-aid program should be reviewed periodically to determine if it continues to address the needs of the specific workplace. Training, supplies, equipment and first-aid policies should be added or modified to account for changes in workplace safety and health hazards, worksite locations and worker schedules since the last program review. The first-aid training program should be kept up-to-date with current first-aid techniques and knowledge. Outdated training and reference materials should be replaced or removed.

Summary

Employers are required by OSHA standard 29 CFR 1910.151 to have a person or persons adequately trained to render first aid for worksites that are not in near proximity to an infirmary, clinic, or hospital.

It is advised that the first-aid program for a particular workplace be designed to reflect the known and anticipated risks of the specific work environment. Consultation with local emergency medical experts and providers of first-aid training is encouraged when developing a first-aid program.

The program must comply with all applicable OSHA standards and regulations. (See section on OSHA Requirements.) OSHA requires certain employers to have CPR-trained rescuers on site.

Sudden cardiac arrest is a potential risk at all worksites, regardless of the type of work. Serious consideration should be given to establishing a workplace AED program.

First-aid supplies must be available in adequate quantities and be readily accessible.

First-aid training courses should include instruction in general and workplace hazard-specific knowledge and skills. CPR training should incorporate AED training if an AED is available at the worksite. First-aid training should be repeated periodically to maintain and update knowledge and skills.

Management commitment and worker involvement is vital in developing, implementing and assessing a workplace first-aid program.

Additional Resources on First Aid, CPR and AEDs

American Association of Occupational Health Nursing at www.aaohn.org

National Safety Council at www.nsc.org

References

American Heart Association. *Heartsaver First Aid with CPR and AED.* Publication 70-2562. Dallas: American Heart Association. 2002.

American Heart Association in collaboration with International Liaison Committee on Resuscitation. *Guidelines 2000 for Cardiopulmonary Resuscitation and Emergency Cardiovascular Care: International Consensus on Science, Part 3: Adult Basic Life Support. Circulation.* 2000; Vol. 102, Supplement I: I 22 - I 59.

American Red Cross. *First Aid: Responding to Emergencies.* Third Edition. 2001.

ANSI Z308.1-2003. *Minimum Requirements for Workplace First Aid Kits.* Arlington VA: International Safety Equipment Association. 2003.

ASTM F2171-02. *Standard Guide for Defining the Performance of First Aid Providers in Occupational Settings.* West Conshohocken, PA. ASTM International. 2002.

Caffrey, S.L., Willoughby, P.J., Pepe, P.E., and Becker, L.B. Public use of automated external defibrillators. *New Eng J Med* 2002; 347(16):1242-47.

ECC Committee, Subcommittees and Task Forces of the American Heart Association. 2005 American Heart Association Guidelines for Cardiopulmonary Resuscitation and Emergency Cardiovascular Care. *Circulation.* 2005 Dec. 13; Vol. 112, Issue 24 Supplement: IV 1-IV 203.

National Guidelines for First Aid Training in Occupational Settings (Revised 2002) 2nd Ed. Available: www.ngfatos.net [June 30, 2004]

National Safety Council. *Injury Facts, 2005 - 2006 Edition.* Itasca, IL (2006).

National Safety Council, *Standard First Aid, CPR and AED,* McGraw-Hill. New York NY. (2005).

U.S. Department of Labor. Bureau of Labor Statistics, Injuries, Illnesses, and Fatalities at www.bls.gov/iif

U.S. Department of Labor. Occupational Safety and Health Administration. Directive CPL 02-02-053. *Guidelines for First Aid Training Programs.* 1991.

OSHA Assistance

OSHA can provide extensive help through a variety of programs, including technical assistance about effective safety and health programs, state plans, workplace consultations, voluntary protection programs, strategic partnerships, training and education, and more. An overall commitment to workplace safety and health can add value to your business, to your workplace and to your life.

Safety and Health Program Management Guidelines

Effective management of worker safety and health protection is a decisive factor in reducing the extent and severity of work-related injuries and illnesses and their related costs. To assist employers and employees in developing effective safety and health programs, OSHA published recommended Safety and Health Program Management Guidelines (54 Federal Register 3904-3916, January 26, 1989). These voluntary guidelines apply to all places of employment covered by OSHA.

The guidelines identify four general elements that are critical to the development of a successful safety and health management program:

Management leadership and employee involvement;

Work analysis;

Hazard prevention and control; and

Safety and health training.

The guidelines recommend specific actions under each of these general elements to achieve an effective safety and health program. The guidelines can be viewed on OSHA's website at www.osha.gov under the heading Federal Registers.

State Programs

The *Occupational Safety and Health Act of 1970* (OSH Act) encourages states to develop and operate their own job safety and health plans. States with plans approved by OSHA under section 18(b) of the OSH Act must adopt standards and enforce require-

ments that are at least as effective as federal requirements. There are currently 26 state plan states: 22 of these administer plans covering both private and public (state and local government) employees; the other plans, Connecticut, New Jersey, New York and the Virgin Islands, cover public sector employees only.

Consultation Services

Consultation assistance is available on request to employers who want help in establishing and maintaining a safe and healthful workplace. Largely funded by OSHA, the service is provided at no cost to the employer. Primarily developed for smaller employers with more hazardous operations, the consultation service is delivered by state governments employing professional safety and health consultants. Comprehensive assistance includes an appraisal of all mechanical systems, work practices and occupational safety and health hazards of the workplace and all aspects of the employer's present job safety and health program.

The program is separate from OSHA's inspection efforts. No penalties are proposed or citations issued for hazards identified by the consultant. The service is confidential. For more information concerning consultation assistance, see the OSHA website at www.osha.gov/dcsp/smallbusiness/consult.html.

Voluntary Protection Programs

Voluntary Protection Programs (VPPs) and onsite consultation services, when coupled with an effective enforcement program, expand worker protection to help meet the goals of the OSH Act. The three levels of VPP—Star, Merit, and Star Demonstration—are designed to recognize outstanding achievement by companies that have successfully incorporated comprehensive safety and health programs into their total management system. The VPPs motivate others to achieve excellent safety and health results in the same outstanding way as they establish a cooperative relationship among employers, employees and OSHA.

For additional information on VPPs and how to apply, visit OSHA's website at: www.osha.gov/dcsp/vpp/index.html or contact your nearest OSHA Area or Regional Office listed at the end of this publication.

Strategic Partnership Program

OSHA's Strategic Partnership Program, the newest of OSHA's cooperative programs, helps encourage, assist and recognize the efforts of partners to eliminate serious workplace hazards and achieve a high level of worker safety and health. Whereas OSHA's Consultation Program and VPP entail one-on-one relationships between OSHA and individual worksites, most strategic partnerships seek to have a broader impact by building cooperative relationships with groups of employers and employees. These partnerships are voluntary, cooperative relationships between OSHA, employers, employee representatives and others (e.g., labor unions, trade and professional associations, universities and other government agencies). For more information on this and other cooperative programs, contact your nearest OSHA office, or visit OSHA's website at www.osha.gov

Alliance Programs

The Alliances Program enables organizations committed to workplace safety and health to collaborate with OSHA to prevent injuries and illnesses in the workplace. OSHA and the Alliance participants work together to reach out to, educate and lead the nation's employers and their employees in improving and advancing workplace safety and health.

Groups that can form an Alliance with OSHA include employers, labor unions, trade or professional groups, educational institutions and government agencies. In some cases, organizations may be building on existing relationships with OSHA through other cooperative programs.

There are few formal program requirements for Alliances and the agreements do not include an enforcement component. However, OSHA and the participating organizations must define, implement and meet a set of short- and long-term goals that fall into three categories: training and education; outreach and communication; and promoting the national dialogue on workplace safety and health.

Training and Education

OSHA's area offices offer a variety of information services, such as compliance assistance, publications, audiovisual aids, technical advice, and speakers for special engagements.

OSHA's Training Institute in Arlington Heights, IL, provides basic and advanced courses in safety and health for federal and state compliance officers, state consultants, federal agency personnel and private sector employers, employees and their representatives.

The OSHA Training Institute also has established OSHA Training Institute Education Centers to address the increased demand for its courses from the private sector and from other federal agencies (see OSHA's website at: www.osha.gov/fso/ote/training/edcenters/index.html). These centers are nonprofit colleges, universities and other organizations that have been selected after a competition for participation in the program.

OSHA also provides funds to nonprofit organizations, through grants, to conduct workplace training and education in subjects where OSHA believes there is a lack of workplace training.

Grants are awarded annually. Grant recipients are expected to contribute 20 percent of the total grant cost.

For more information on grants, training and education, contact the OSHA Training Institute, Office of Training and Education, on OSHA's website at: www.osha.gov/dcsp/ote/index.html, or at 2020 South Arlington Heights Road, Arlington Heights, IL 60005-4102, (847) 297-4810, Fax (847) 297-4874. For further information on any OSHA program, contact your nearest OSHA area or regional office listed at the end of this publication.

Information Available Electronically

OSHA has a variety of materials and tools available on its website at www.osha.gov. These include e-Tools such as Expert Advisors, Electronic Compliance Assistance Tools (e-cats), Technical Links; regulations, directives and publications; videos and other information for employers and employees. OSHA's software programs and compliance assistance tools walk you

through challenging safety and health issues and common problems to find the best solutions for your workplace.

A wide variety of OSHA materials, including standards, interpretations, directives, and more, can be purchased on CD-ROM from the U.S. Government Printing Office, Superintendent of Documents, phone toll-free (866) 512-1800.

OSHA Publications

OSHA has an extensive publications program. For a listing of free or sales items, visit OSHA's website at www.osha.gov or contact the OSHA Publications Office, U.S. Department of Labor, 200 Constitution Avenue, NW, N-3101, Washington, DC 20210. Telephone (202) 693-1888 or fax to (202) 693-2498.

Contacting OSHA

To report an emergency, file a complaint or seek OSHA advice, assistance or products, call (800) 321-OSHA or contact your nearest OSHA regional or area office listed below. The teletypewriter (TTY) number is (877) 889-5627.

You can also file a complaint online and obtain more information on OSHA federal and state programs by visiting OSHA's website at www.osha.gov.

For further information on any OSHA program, contact your nearest OSHA area or regional office listed at the end of this publication.

OSHA Regional Offices

Region I
(CT,* ME, MA, NH, RI, VT*)
JFK Federal Building, Room E340
Boston, MA 02203
(617) 565-9860

Region II
(NJ,* NY,* PR,* VI*)
201 Varick Street, Room 670
New York, NY 10014
(212) 337-2378

Region III
(DE, DC, MD,* PA, VA,* WV)
The Curtis Center
170 S. Independence Mall West
Suite 740 West
Philadelphia, PA 19106-3309
(215) 861-4900

Region IV
(AL, FL, GA, KY,* MS, NC,* SC,* TN*)
61 Forsyth Street, SW
Atlanta, GA 30303
(404) 562-2300

Region V
(IL, IN,* MI,* MN,* OH, WI)
230 South Dearborn Street
Room 3244
Chicago, IL 60604
(312) 353-2220

Region VI
(AR, LA, NM,* OK, TX)
525 Griffin Street, Room 602
Dallas, TX 75202
(214) 767-4731 or 4736 x224

Region VII
(IA,* KS, MO, NE)
City Center Square
1100 Main Street, Suite 800
Kansas City, MO 64105
(816) 426-5861

Region VIII
(CO, MT, ND, SD, UT,* WY*)
1999 Broadway, Suite 1690
PO Box 46550
Denver, CO 80202-5716
(720) 264-6550

Region IX
(American Samoa, AZ,* CA,* HI,* NV,*
Northern Mariana Islands)
71 Stevenson Street, Room 420
San Francisco, CA 94105
(415) 975-4310

Region X
(AK,* ID, OR,* WA*)
1111 Third Avenue, Suite 715
Seattle, WA 98101-3212
(206) 553-5930

* These 26 states and territories operate their own OSHA-approved job safety and health programs (Connecticut, New Jersey, New York and the Virgin Islands plans cover public employees only). States with approved programs must have standards that are identical to, or at least as effective as, the Federal OSHA standards.

Note: To get contact information for OSHA Area Offices, OSHA-approved State Plans and OSHA Consultation Projects, please visit us online at www.osha.gov or call us at 1-800-321-OSHA.

Employers are responsible for providing a safe and healthful workplace for their employees. OSHA's role is to assure the safety and health of America's workers by setting and enforcing standards; providing training, outreach and education; establishing partnerships; and encouraging continual improvement in workplace safety and health.

This handbook provides a general overview of a particular topic related to OSHA standards. It does not alter or determine compliance responsibilities in OSHA standards or the *Occupational Safety and Health Act of 1970*. Because interpretations and enforcement policy may change over time, you should consult current OSHA administrative interpretations and decisions by the Occupational Safety and Health Review Commission and the Courts for additional guidance on OSHA compliance requirements.

This information is available to sensory impaired individuals upon request. Voice phone: (202) 693-1999; teletypewriter (TTY) number: (877) 889-5627.